DOÑA FELISA

"Love, not politics, is what
gets things done."

—Felisa Rincón de Gautier

Other books by Marianna Norris

FATHER AND SON FOR FREEDOM

YOUNG INDIA

YOUNG TURKEY

DOÑA FELISA

A Biography
of the Mayor of San Juan

MARIANNA NORRIS

Illustrated with photographs

DODD, MEAD & COMPANY
NEW YORK

To my mother

The dialogue in this book is as reported by
those involved or taken from their writings.

Library of Congress Catalog Card Number: 69-15557

Printed in the United States of America
by The Cornwall Press, Inc., Cornwall, N. Y.

Acknowledgments

The author gratefully acknowledges the help of the following persons:

Ricardo Alegría, Yvonne Alejandro, María Alvarez, Dr. Rafael Arrillaga Torrens, Rosita Auffant, Josefina O. de Batlle, Emma Boehm Oller, José A. Buitrago, Antonio Colorado, Eliseo Combas Guerra, Señora José F. Correa, Carmen Delgado, Juan Díaz Peralta, Ernesto Juan Fonfrías, Jorge Font Saldaña, Carmen de Font Saldaña, Camilo Fraticelli, Genaro Gautier, Vicente Geigel-Polanco, Margaret Greer, Robert G. Greer, Samuel Halper, Lucille Hoshabjian, Mercedes Iglesias, Luis Laboy, Joel Magruder, Monina Mendoza de González, Joseph Monserrat, Luis Muñoz Rivera, Muna Muñoz Lee, Miguel Angel Nater, María Negrón Muñoz, Cremilda Ocasio, Catalina Palerm, María Esilda Rincón de Palerm, Mac Phillips, Rita Rincón de Pietrantoni, Pedro Puig Nater, Clara Luz Vizcarrondo de Quiñones, Samuel R. Quiñones, Luis Ramírez, Enrique Ramírez Brau, Supreme Court Justice Marco Rigau, Fini Rincón, Rita Angélica Rincón de Rubiano, Paula Carbana de Rivera, Carlos

5

Acknowledgments

Romero Barceló, Zaida Rosa, Inocencio Sepúlveda, José Antonio Sepúlveda, Helen Tooker, José Arsenio Torres, Lee Volker, Sandra Young.

Contents

7

Illustrations

9

Illustrations

Prologue

THE RINCÓNS' maid had not come that morning and Don Enrique sent his daughter Felisa to see if the woman was sick.

She walked through the blue brick streets of Old San Juan. Wrought-iron balconies, palm trees seen through arched doorways—it was all familiar until she came to La Perla. The slum clung to a cliff between San Juan and the Atlantic, far below. Most people never did more than look down at the roofs of La Perla. But on this day, Felisa walked on down the stone steps. She was wearing jasmine in her hair, breathing in the perfume. Then, suddenly, the fragrance of jasmine was gone and the smell of death was all around her.

She shuddered. Then the wind brought the bellow of dying cattle and she understood. The city slaughter-house was somewhere down there to windward of the slum.

She started down again toward the maid's house. The

11

street was only a few feet wide, steep and muddy. A rat ran freely across her path. Skinny children stared at her. They called shrilly and their mothers came to the doorways to look, too. Felisa wanted to greet the women with the traditional politeness of Puerto Rico, but the gaunt tragedy of their faces shriveled her smile.

Where the street turned, the rocks fell away to the sea and she saw the sharks. Drawn from miles away by the smell of blood from the slaughterhouse, they circled and leaped in frenzy.

She began to run between the decaying wooden shacks, slipping and sliding in the mud. The children, excited, were running after her. The screams of the doomed cattle were louder down here and the death wind choked her.

Suddenly, she was crying and crossing herself because here on the edge of her own city she had stumbled into a nightmare.

At home, that night, she was unable to sleep. She relived the walk through La Perla, saw again the tumbledown board shack where she had found the maid. She thought of how many, many shacks there were and how many other slums, acres and miles of them, across the face of San Juan.

The poverty of Puerto Rico was a problem even statesmen couldn't solve. What could a woman do about it? In Puerto Rico, in the 1920's, a woman couldn't even vote. Her function was to stay home and obey her father until she had a husband to obey. What could a woman do?

In the dark night, Felisa Rincón folded her hands and prayed to God that she might find a way to bring help to the suffering poor.

"Softly, Softly!"

"SOFTLY, SOFTLY!" Felisa Rincón's mother always told her. Doña Rita Rincón was a beautiful, delicate woman who never raised her voice.

She was a teacher and Felisa was almost born in the schoolhouse of the tiny Puerto Rican town of Ceiba. Doña Rita just got home in time. After Felisa, she had three more daughters and set about raising them all to be ladies.

"Straight, straight!" she would say to make them sit up, and "Softly, softly!" to make them gentle and feminine.

That was fine with Enrique Rincón, her husband. Like most Puerto Ricans at the turn of the century, he admired the old-fashioned virtues in women. Don Enrique was tall and thin, with fine features. His friends told him he looked like Don Quixote whom he so often quoted.

A lawyer by profession, a liberal in politics, Don Enrique was a restless soul. He moved his law practice often. The family was living in Humacao, on the green eastern end of Puerto Rico, when his wife told him they were to have another child.

Don Enrique loved his daughters, Felisa, Josefina, Cecilia, and María Esilda. But the old Spanish tradition was strong in him and for years he had longed for a son.

Felisa heard her mother praying to St. Ramón for a boy, this time. Her prayers were answered and the baby was named Ramón after the saint.

Two more boys, Enrique and Gallego, came later. Doña Rita was not strong. When Gallego was born, the doctor worked and worried over her but her strength ebbed and the moment came when he could feel no pulse.

"She's dead," the doctor said.

His hand stayed on her pulse and then, faintly, he felt it stir. She lived and recovered but the doctor warned her, "No more children."

The ones she had kept her busy enough. While Papa taught the boys to be manly, Mama taught the girls how to run a house gracefully. Felisa, being the oldest, got most of the instruction.

Even when things were going well for the Rincóns and they had servants, the girls were required to keep up their cooking and sewing and to wash and iron one piece of their own clothing each week, just to polish their skill in the household arts. They did it all with "Softly, softly!" ringing in their ears.

Doña Felisa

Father took care of training their minds. He read to them each night, after dinner. Don Quixote and other Spanish classics, of course. And the Bible, explaining it carefully as he went along. The older girls, Felisa and Josefina, would sit on either side of the oil lamp, embroidering with fine stitches as they listened to the rolling verses.

"No more children!" the doctor had told Doña Rita when Gallego was born. After they moved to Santurce, a suburb of San Juan, she learned she was to have another baby. She grew quiet and sombre-eyed.

One day, she asked Felisa to help her cut out the school clothes for the following season for all the children. When the job was finished, she took her smallest daughter, María Esilda, in her lap and prayed for a long time.

That night, another daughter, Rita, was born and Doña Rita, the mother, died. Don Enrique had to break the news to the children.

Felisa stood, mute and suffering, until the little ones started to cry. Then she knew what she must do.

She folded them to her. "Softly . . . softly . . ." she said.

II

La Cerámica

THE CHILDREN were playing among the orange trees in the yard. Felisa could hear them chanting.

> Doña Ana, Doña Ana isn't here.
> She's out in the garden, my dear.
> She's opening roses,
> And closing carnations.
> She's busy, this time of the year!

The Rincóns were living on a farm, near Vega Baja, in a rambling two-story farmhouse with a big open tank on the roof to catch rainwater. The former owners had made pottery and the place was still called La Cerámica.

Don Enrique loved farming. The profits from his law practice usually went into his farms. Here, he had forty acres of tobacco and pineapples, some banana and cashew trees, and three acres of flowers.

Felisa loved it but, like Doña Ana in the children's song, she was a very busy person. The Rincón children —half of them blonde, like their father, who had French

17

blood, the others Spanish brunettes like their mother—were a gay unpredictable brood.

Josefina (she was always called Fini) was fair—a brainy, spirited girl.

Cecilia was a brunette and an adventurer. She kept Felisa running as she looked always for new places to explore, new things to do. Like the saint for whom she was named, Cecilia was musical. She sang and played the piano and the mandolin.

Silin (that was María Esilda's nickname) was blonde and naughty. Sometimes Felisa grabbed a poppy switch and spanked her legs with it. Sometimes she made her kneel in front of the statue of Jesus and pray to be a good girl.

Ramón, usually called Moncho, was his father's favorite and made the most of it. Sometimes he would storm at the girls, "When Papa is out, *I* am the head of the family and you must do as I say!"

The girls acknowledged his principle—women had few rights in Puerto Rico in those days—but in practice they were unlikely to obey him.

"Yes, you are the head of the family," Felisa would answer, "but in the meantime, would you please . . ."

The younger children, Enrique, Gallego, and Rita, were just about big enough to chase the white egrets that flew low over the fields and to pester the farmhand at milking time for a squirt of warm milk straight from the cow.

Felisa, since the day she sat down at the sewing machine to finish that first batch of school clothes, had been their mother. She fed them and clothed them, sang them to sleep at night, and sent them to school in the morning.

As for her own education, after the third year of high school, her father had taken her out, saying she was needed at home. The Rincóns were never really poor. But somehow they were never rich enough so that Felisa could be spared to finish her schooling.

Don Enrique married again. His wife was charming, but not accustomed to housework. She played the piano while Felisa continued to run the house. When Manolin was born, and then a second half-brother, Felisa had two more to take care of.

She was an artist at homemaking. In the kitchen, her specialty was *asopao,* Puerto Rican stew. She made it out of chicken or turkey or sometimes goat, marinated in lemon, with olives and whole tomatoes and onions and plenty of garlic, because Papa loved garlic.

Felisa's uncle was a pharmacist. For a while, she went to stay with him to learn his profession. But when she was almost ready to take the examination, her father again decreed that she was needed at home.

The peasants in the neighborhood—the *jíbaros,* Puerto Ricans call them—were as glad as her own family to have her back. She had always fed them when they were hungry, which was often, and nursed them when they were sick. There were no doctors out in the country, and Felisa had a knack for healing that was often needed. Out to the thatched wooden shacks she would rush, her dark braids flying, whenever a child had a fever, or a father was hurt in a machete accident in the fields. She bound wounds, gave injections, and prescribed freely. If it was a matter of life or death, she sent to town for the doctor. When the teen-age girl sent word that he must come right away, the doctor dropped everything and made the long trip to the country, for he knew her judgment was sound.

Many a night, an anxious peasant hammered on the Rincóns' door, calling to Felisa that his wife was about to have a baby. Felisa lost track of how many births she had assisted.

Times were hard for the *jíbaros*. They depended on the sugar plantations for a living and there was just not enough work. (A good Puerto Rican, people used to say, puts three spoons of sugar in his coffee—two for sweetness and one to help the industry.) Things were bad enough in the harvest season. The cane cutters worked fifteen or sixteen hours for only forty cents a day. But much of the year they would walk the miles to the Sugar Central in the morning only to find that there was no work at all.

As they trudged past La Cerámica on their way to the Central each morning, the *jíbaros* found a friend waiting for them. Felisa would be there at the door with hot, strong Puerto Rican coffee to brace them for the long hike.

Puerto Ricans like to make up songs, and the *jíbaros* made up verses about Felisa and sang them.

La Cerámica

Felisa, niñita, you never forget us!
Felisa, chiquita, your coffee's so good!

So they sang as they walked the dusty Puerto Rican
roads to the jobs that might not be there.

Felisa had little life away from the farm. On Wednesday, the Rincóns piled into the carriage and visited rela-
tives. On Sunday, they went to church. Those were their
outings. It had to be something very important before
Father would take them out on a Saturday. Don Enrique
did not care for his girls going to parties.

Felisa enjoyed Saturday anyway, for that was the day
she made her desserts. In the big kitchen, she could be
found preparing puddings, fruit, and cake for the whole
week.

"Let's see . . . *flan* tonight. Tomorrow, *lechosa* . . .
Then guava shells, Wednesday. Thursday, maybe man-
goes in syrup . . ."

She could hear the children in the yard, chanting a
Puerto Rican counting-out rhyme.

Peck, bird, peck!
Peck and seek!
Who gave you
That big, big beak?

From the parlor, a popular song floated in. Stirring
the *flan,* a thick Spanish custard, Felisa hummed softly
along with the piano. The second Señora Rincón played
beautifully.

21

III

————◆————

"Alegría, Alegría!"

Alegría, alegría, alegría!
Alegría, alegría and joy!
For Mary has gone to the stable
To have her little boy!

Don Enrique put down his guitar and took up his
flute as the whole family joined in singing the *aguinaldos*
—Spanish Christmas carols.

Christmas for the Rincóns was the high spot of the
year, the final symbol of their warm, close family life
and their joy in being together.

Both father and mother came from big families, so
there were hordes of aunts, uncles, and cousins on hand.

On Noche Buena, Christmas Eve, even the children
were allowed to stay up for midnight Mass. The next
day the feast of the year took place.

Out in the garden, a pig was roasted. *Pasteles*, little
rolled pies of banana or sweet potato, went with it, and

morcillas, tidbits of stuffed tripe. Dessert was a special sweet milk pudding.

A family *trulla,* a group of musicians playing old Puerto Rican guitars, scratchers, and percussion sticks, would keep the *aguinaldos* going all day. "Saludos, Saludos" and "Shepherds, Come," "Give Me Cakes" and "The Gates of Bethlehem"—they sang them all.

Felisa had decorated the house with scarlet poinsettias and a beautiful nativity scene. Her hair wound with fragrant *mosito* flowers, she was everywhere at once, filling cups with *coquito,* the holiday rum and coconut drink, and seeing that everyone got some *turrón,* the crisp Christmas candy from Spain.

Christmas was the Rincóns' own holiday but Don Enrique, being a convivial man, continued his entertaining through the whole year. His guests were of varying races, creeds, and talents. The most frequent visitors were his law partners.

Luis Llorens Torres was a distinguished civil lawyer. He also happened to be one of Puerto Rico's finest poets. When he finally gave in to his destiny and left the law, his poems were already known all over the Spanish-speaking world.

Nemesio Canales, besides being a lawyer, wrote humor. Like Llorens Torres, he later gave up law to devote himself to literature. Canales, a socialist and an unconventional philosopher, deplored the stodgy state of the island's society and felt that he was too much ahead of his time to be appreciated. He was right. For a time, he

Doña Felisa

was a member of the island legislature. When he proposed giving the vote to women, his fellow legislators ridiculed him.

Llorens, Canales, and other intellectuals would often drop in at the farm for an evening of talk or a week end of duck-hunting.

Don Enrique's teen-age daughters were quick-witted and well read. They took a full part in the older men's conversation, whether it dealt with the troubles of the *jíbaros* or the philosophy of Swedenborg, whom Papa greatly admired. Though the girls seldom left the confines of the farm, their minds ranged the world with these thinkers, poets, and lawmakers.

After a day's hunting, the company would take up their guitars and sing, improvising jibes at each other in verse. The girls came in for their share of teasing. Of Fini's tousled blonde hair, the poets sang:

> You can't tell what it is,
> The hair of Josefine!
> A shock of corn?
> A hen's nest?
> Or something in between!

A very elderly neighbor asked Don Enrique for Felisa's hand in marriage, and brought forth another song.

> The day Felisa marries
> She'll take Cecilia, too.
> To prop the poor old bridegroom up
> 'Til he can say "I do."

24

"Alegría, Alegría!"

Llorens and the others frequently joked about the restrictions Rincón put on his daughters. After his second wife died, Enrique isolated the girls more than ever.

"You have no chaperone for yourself," his friends sang to him, "but, oh, how careful you are with your girls!"

Felisa was too busy to be rebellious but, more and more, Fini questioned the rules that hemmed them in. Why couldn't she join them for duck-hunting, she wanted to know. Moncho who was little more than a child went along on the jaunts across the countryside, but she had to stay at home helping get dinner ready. Why?

One day, she took a gun from the closet and went out on her own, to hunt. She had never touched a gun before but she aimed at a bird, pulled the trigger and, to her shocked surprise, found a dead bird on her hands. She had asserted her equality, but it was a hollow victory.

Nights when Papa was not at home working on the treatise he was writing about the Bible, he tended to be out late with his friends. On those nights, a black servant, Segundo, sat under the mango tree in front of the house, holding a shotgun in his lap. Segundo had his orders. No visitors.

With prior permission, a young man might drop in for exactly thirty minutes. But not many qualified for permission. Once, one of the lawyers brought a handsome young Spaniard to the house and a spark of love

25

flew between him and Felisa. Papa observed, and put his foot down. The young man was no longer welcome at La Cerámica. When he returned to Spain and never wrote to Felisa, she rationalized that it was just as well. Look how quickly he had forgotten her. Father had known best, as usual. But underneath, she had a deep hunger to move out into the great world beyond the farmhouse.

Fini and Felisa shared a bedroom on the second floor. The last thing at night, Felisa would make the rounds of the children's cots to see that they were all bathed and brushed and well tucked in. After she heard the last of their prayers, she turned down the lamp and went to bed.

Nights at Vega Baja were full of the fragrance of cane flowers and roses, gardenias and jasmine. In the blackness, the melodious call of the *coqui*, the tiny Puerto Rican tree frog, would sound. *Co-qui . . . Co-qui . . .* its note as sweet and lyrical as a bird call.

And then, sometimes, there would be another sound —a guitar playing and a voice under the window singing about love.

> You are my heart, you are my life,
> How can I tell you what I feel . . .

Some neighbor boy was pouring his heart into his song for one of the girls.

The children in the next room were sleeping. Listening in the dark, the girls could hear their even breath-

"Alegría, Alegría!"

ing. But Felisa and Fini knew that, across the hall, their father was awake. Downstairs, Segundo was awake and listening, too.

In the old tradition of Spain, a lady has one answer to a voice in the night under her window. She may not speak or show herself. She may not drop a flower or throw a kiss. The girls knew the code only too well.

Quietly, Felisa sat up in bed and reached for the oil lamp. She lit a match, put it to the wick, and replaced the chimney. Light filled the room. Through the curtains, some of the light shone outside. That was the only sign of recognition they could give.

The song ended and another began . . . "Love, your name is a crystal bell . . ."

Arm in arm, fair head and dark leaning against each other, the two girls listened to the songs in silence.

IV

———◆■◆———

The Angel

MONCHO WAS furious.

"You're lying," he told his friend. "My sister is not at that beach party! She is not allowed to leave the house alone!"

His friend shrugged. There was no use in making Moncho any angrier.

The beach parties were harmless enough. Families went down together to roast pork and sing around the fire every Saturday night. For the young people, it was the big event of the week. But Don Enrique had never let his family indulge in that type of merrymaking.

Not that they hadn't suggested it. Fini, especially, argued hotly that they should be allowed to go. What was wrong with it? But arguing with Papa never did much good and, in the end, she subsided.

One Saturday, Fini announced sadly that her dear friend, Concha, was not feeling well. Father gave her permission to visit the girl and take her some pastries

Felisa had made. He walked Fini to the girl's house himself.

He was deep in his scholarly writing, later in the evening, when teen-age Moncho came in like a hurricane.

"Where is she? Where is Fini?"

"She is passing a few hours with Concha."

"She's not at home? Then it's true. They told me my sister was at the beach party, tossing her hair, and waving her fan and singing."

Papa stiffened.

"I'll go and get her," said Moncho. "I'll go down there and bring her home where she belongs!"

And he stormed out of the house.

Moncho rose late the next morning. The girls were already at the breakfast table when he hurried in and took his place.

He grinned as he reached for the milk pitcher.

"Fini," he said, "you almost caught it from me last night."

Fini munched on her *tostada*.

"Some fellow told me he saw you at the beach party. Was I furious! I ran down there to get you. Lucky for you, you weren't there."

Fini put down her *tostada*. There was a glint in her blue eyes.

"I was there. Concha felt much better and we both went down there with her aunt and uncle. Someone warned me that you were coming and I hid. I was hiding when you stormed around there making a fool of yourself looking for me!"

Her father rose and she whirled on him. "And what's more, I'm going again next week. Why not? Why not, Papa?"

Felisa jumped up. "Quietly!" she said. But she turned to her father, too. "Everyone goes, Papa. What's wrong with a family party where everyone in town goes?"

Don Enrique stared at his two daughters—tall, fiery, demanding his answer. He saw that they were not children but young women.

He sat down at the table again and signaled them all to do the same. When they had retrieved fallen napkins and resumed their places, he spoke.

"Moncho, it's no use. We'll go next Saturday. We'll take the girls." He turned to his oldest daughter. "Felisa, you'll prepare a supper for us to take along."

The Inaugural Ball was a very different matter. Not only did the girls know that their father would never take them to celebrate the new governor's inauguration but, like Cinderella, they had nothing to wear to such an affair even if he would hear of it.

Only a few of their friends were going, a few lucky ones. After church, for several Sundays, the girls had gathered in envious groups around the privileged few, hearing details of the ball gowns they were having made

The Angel

for the occasion. (There were no such things as ready-made ball gowns in Puerto Rico then.)

There would be a famous orchestra, and the girls swooped around in waltz steps imagining the thrill of such an occasion. Besides the waltz and the two-step, they would do the old traditional *danza* of Puerto Rico, a romantic suite in which the gentleman introduces himself to the lady, takes her fan and gallantly fans her with it, then dances her off. At such a ball they would even do the *lanceros*, a gay, French-descended dance in which twelve couples salute and change partners in graceful, complicated patterns. The girls practiced the dances and dreamed.

The Rincóns were late getting their tobacco crop in that year. Tobacco spoils if it is not shipped out quickly, so Felisa was seated in the big farmhouse kitchen helping the workers sort the leaves. There were heaps of the brown-gold tobacco everywhere.

Usually, the *jíbaros* brought their guitars to work with them and one or another would take a rest from sorting and play while the others worked. Suddenly, the front door slammed and Don Enrique was calling the girls.

Felisa and Fini arrived at the same time.

"Here." He shoved giant boxes at them. "You're going to the Inaugural Ball."

They were dumbstruck for a moment and then they tore open the cardboard and tissue.

Felisa took out a shining white ball gown, trailing

chiffon and gleaming with silver. Blonde Fini was hugging a gown of blue.

"Oh, they talked me into it," Don Enrique was explaining. "Llorens and Canales and the rest."

His partners were always telling him that he didn't let his girls get out enough. Stung by their criticism, he had brought their measurements to the best modiste in San Juan to get the gowns made so that he could take them to the Inaugural Ball.

Felisa, her heart pounding, ran upstairs with her dress and the dainty white dancing shoes that had been tucked into the box with it.

The *jíbaros* were working away quietly when one old man happened to look up. His jaw dropped.

"*Dios mío!*" he gasped. "An angel!" He dropped to his knees and crossed himself.

The others followed his gaze to the head of the stairs where a figure stood, all in white, glittering with silver.

"An angel?" another shouted. "No, it's our Felisa!"

Smiling radiantly, the angel came down the steps.

"I'm going to the ball," she said. "I'm going to the Inaugural Ball!"

They stood gaping at their friend, their nurse, their coffee-maker, in this miraculous garb, her dark hair piled high like a lady.

Then someone grabbed a guitar. "Show us how you will dance at the great fiesta, Felisa!" he cried.

Picking up her huge skirt delicately, she pointed her white satin toe and danced and danced, showing them

The city of San Juan with the fortress of El Morro in the foreground

Felisa Rincón in her twenties

Below: Part of La Perla slum

Felisa as a young political worker

Below: Felisa and her husband,
Genaro Gautier

Felisa greets her sister, Fini, at the airport

The towers of San Juan City Hall

Puerto Rico Information Service

The Mayor of San Juan in her office. Behind her, the San Juan coat-of-arms, granted by King Ferdinand in 1511.

Felisa and her husband, Genaro, in Washington, D.C.

Felisa Rincón

New garbage trucks arriving in San Juan

The Mayor in a dress she designed and made from a Spanish mantilla

Felisa with Eleanor Roosevelt

Felisa's beach house at Vega Baja

Left: Visiting a construction project, the Mayor wears a regulation safety helmet. *Below:* Felisa helps celebrate Air Force Day.

Right: The Mayor of San Juan visits the Mayor of New York City. *Below:* Campaigning in New York, Felisa takes time out to visit a child care center.

Archivo El Mundo

Archivo El Mundo

Puerto Rico Information Service

Christmas in San Juan

Religious tradition prescribes a bath in the sea on San Juan Day, June 24. Felisa gets her dunking at the Caribe Hilton beach.

Caribe Hilton

Archivo El Mundo

Felisa keeps in touch with the citizens, wherever they live

Archivo El Mundo

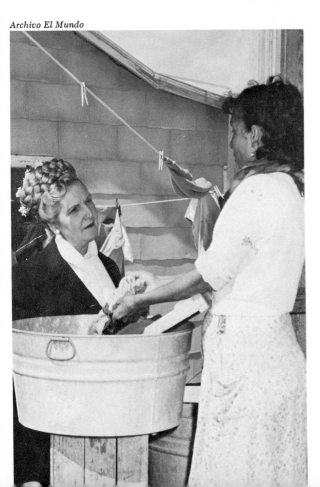

Felisa with Samuel
Quiñones

Archivo El Mundo

Celebrating San Juan Day with Jorge Font Saldaña, Secretary of the Treasury

Caribe Hilton

The Mayor dances
with constituents

Archivo El Mundo

Puerto Rico Information Service

One of the Mayor's favorite projects—restoration of the Old City. Blue-bricked Cristo Street leads to a seventeenth-century chapel.

The Angel

the *lanceros* and the *danza* and the waltz and everything
else she knew, to the sound of clapping and the cries of
Ole! Ole!, there among the brown-gold heaps of tobacco, in the big country kitchen of the Rincón farmhouse.

"I Am Going to Disobey You"

"I AM GOING to disobey you," Felisa told her father. "I have never disobeyed you before, but today I will."

Don Enrique stared at her in disbelief. Felisa was in her thirties. But, in the Spanish tradition, an unmarried lady of any age is still subject to her father's rule.

It was 1932 and Puerto Rican women had just won the right to vote.

"No daughter of mine will ever vote," Don Enrique had said. But the poverty and suffering that Felisa had seen in both city and country had been a weight in her heart for years and she wanted to do something about them.

When the first shock at her show of defiance wore off, Don Enrique began to smile.

"It's true that you've never disobeyed me," he said. "Voting must be very important to you. Well, if it means that much to you, I shall take you to the poll myself."

They were living in San Juan again. Felisa hurried

"I Am Going to Disobey You"

down with her father to the polling place. Standing in line, she looked around curiously. It was the first glorious day of woman suffrage, but the women were not voting. She was the only one in line.

Antonio Barceló, leader of the Liberal Party, was a friend of the Rincóns and Fini's godfather. When he arrived, Felisa pointed out the lack of women voters.

"I appoint you chairman of the Women's Committee," Don Antonio told her. "See if you can get some ladies down here to vote!"

Felisa started at the head of the street, ringing bells and asking women to vote. They were aghast at her suggestion.

"Felisa, it isn't ladylike!"

"Felisa! You didn't! *My* father would never allow it!"

"My husband wouldn't hear of it!"

She went to every house on the block, urging, persuading. At the end of the street, she had nothing but refusals.

Then she had a thought. She walked back to the first house and rang the bell again. Her friend opened the door.

"Now, I told you, Felisa . . ."

Felisa said, "Of course, dear! But may I speak to your maid?"

She went to every house again, urging the maids to vote. As they hurried to the poll, their disgruntled mistresses hurried after them. There was a fine turnout of women voters.

35

Doña Felisa

A week after women got the vote in Puerto Rico, Felisa Rincón was appointed to the Executive Committee of the Liberal Party.

She was in politics.

VI

——◆——

"Bread, Land, Liberty"

FATHER SAID no.

The Liberal Party wanted Felisa to run for the legislature but he would not hear of it.

Fini and her cousin, María Alvarez, were both pressing him for permission to go to law school. (María's father being dead, Enrique was acting head of her family, too.) He said no to Fini and María as he had to Felisa.

When all three dynamic young ladies demanded permission to visit New York, Don Enrique decided he'd better say yes for a change.

Felisa had long thought of starting her own dress shop. She could design as well as sew and turned out a trousseau for each girl in the family who married. Now, she wanted to learn the tricks of the professionals.

Kiviette Fashions in New York was a paradise for anyone who loved beautiful clothes. The girls were hired to embroider beads and sequins on ball gowns that would be sold to Fifth Avenue shops and bought by millionaires.

One day, with a thousand-dollar gown at stake, the designer failed to show up. Mrs. Kiviette was frantic. Felisa volunteered to make the dress.

An untried embroiderer? Mrs. Kiviette was dubious.

"Watch," said Felisa. "I'll do it without cutting the material and you can see how you like it."

Her fingers flew with the pins, shaping, draping the rich material. The whole shop gathered around to watch. When she was finished, Mrs. Kiviette studied the gown.

"Cut it!" she said. "You've got the job!"

Felisa saw her first snow that year. At Christmas, since all the girls in the shop were Puerto Rican, they brought in *pasteles* and *morcillos* and sang *aguinaldos*.

"To fame and fortune in New York!" someone toasted, raising a glass of *coquito*. "Felisa, you're going straight to the top in this business!"

But home ties were too strong for Felisa. A few months later, she was back in San Juan with her family.

Felisa's Style Shop opened its doors on the Plaza Colón, at the entrance to the Old City. Business was good, immediately. The wives of the rich plantation owners flocked to buy her original designs. But other things were going on in San Juan that were more important to Felisa Rincón than her ball gowns.

The one issue that had always divided Puerto Ricans

38

into armed camps was the island's status in relation to the United States. Some Puerto Ricans wanted statehood. The wealthy—the big plantation owners—saw this as the one way to protect their property from the political turmoil that plagued the rest of Latin America. But other Puerto Ricans wanted independence. The United States, they said, had failed to solve the island's problems. It was time to let Puerto Ricans work out their own destiny as a free country.

While statehooders and *independentistas* fought among themselves, disease and hunger and illiteracy spread on the island. More and more small farmers were losing their farms to the big sugar companies. The dispossessed *jíbaros* went to the city to find work. There was none, and they ended up in the spreading slums.

Life expectancy on the Mainland was sixty years. On the island of Puerto Rico, it was only forty-two years. A Congressional committee, appointed to study conditions on the island, reported that its problems were "insoluble."

Suddenly, a new leader appeared. Luis Muñoz Marín was the son of Muñoz Rivera, a poet-statesman who had fought for Puerto Rico's freedom from Spain.

At first, young Muñoz and Antonio Barceló worked together in the Liberal Party, with Felisa and Fini among their hard-working aides. But shrewd enemies fostered misunderstanding between the new young leader and the older one and, in the end, Muñoz and his supporters were put out of the Liberal Party. The

Doña Felisa

Rincóns loved Barceló, but they followed Muñoz, for they shared a growing feeling that he was the man who could save their stricken island.

To start a new political party was a staggering task. They would have to get more than 50,000 signatures from all over the island, each witnessed by a judge, just to get on the ballot. Muñoz decided to try.

He knew one thing. Puerto Ricans could no longer afford to fight with each other over status.

"We'll call a truce on status so we can work together on our real problems," he said. "Instead of fighting each other, we'll join to fight poverty and disease."

For Muñoz' new Popular Democratic Party, the basic issue would be land reform. If elected, they would buy land from the big sugar corporations and give it back to the peasants who had lost it. They would pass social legislation to bring health and education to the poor. And they would start industries so that there would be jobs for those who had no land.

All her life, Felisa Rincón had ministered to the poor. She wept at the thought of what these social measures could mean to them.

Elections came every fourth year in Puerto Rico. The Popular Party had two years to establish itself and win over the voters. But it had one big problem. The poor people—the voters the Populars hoped to win—had never participated in a democratic election. Under the Spaniards, they had had no vote. Under the Americans, they had the right to vote but no one had ever trained them in democracy or showed them what the vote could mean. For them, elections were a form, only. The wealthy sugar owners paid them two dollars each and told them how to vote.

The system had been entrenched for years. It never occurred to the poor that it might be changed. After centuries of oppression, they accepted poverty as the will of God and accepted two dollars on election day to vote as they were told. In the two years before the next election, the new party had to overcome the old way of doing things and implant the concept that the vote is a powerful weapon which men can use to better their lives.

The Populars began to hold rallies in the villages. Muñoz Marín, big, dark, fiery, would climb up on a sugar cane cart and speak to the straw-hatted *jíbaros*.

"Lend me your vote," he would say. "Don't give it to me. Just lend it to me this once. Then watch me. And watch your own cooking pot. If things are better, you can keep me in office. If they are not, you can take back your vote again and sell it to the other party at the next election.

"Try it," he advised them. "You can only lose two dollars. And you might win health, education, and a future for your children!"

The slogan of the Popular Party was "Self-respect versus Money." But the *jíbaros* had been deceived so many times in the past. They had a traditional distrust of politicians, of city people, of educated people. It was

41

hard to tell what they were thinking. The Populars could only keep campaigning and hope that the people would believe them.

They had another slogan. *Jalda Arriba!* . . . Up the Hill! Someone set it to music and to its rousing march they climbed the hills of Puerto Rico with their message of social justice.

Felisa was chairman of the party's Municipal Committee. Her responsibility—the city of San Juan. The "haves" in San Juan already belonged to other political parties. Her job was to bring the Popular Party message to the "have nots."

To Felisa, "Up the Hill!" meant up the cliff of La Perla. She went up and down it daily, carrying the words of Muñoz Marín and the banner of the new party. It was a white and red banner bearing the profile of a *jíbaro* in a straw hat. The words on it . . . Bread, Land, Liberty.

VII

————◆————

"Get Out If You Can"

FELISA RINCÓN went every morning to kneel in the San Juan Cathedral and pray for the success of the Popular Party. Then she walked down toward the Old City walls and her work.

The walls were of native limestone, thirty feet thick. Once, they had surrounded the whole city, making it a great bastion to protect the Spanish treasure fleets that plied the Caribbean. In the 1930's, they marked a ring of slums, teeming with rats and hungry humans.

Felisa had discovered La Perla that day the maid was sick. She was to explore many more slums before the election.

Where once the Old City's Land Gate, Puerta de Tierra, had stood, the wall had crumbled, leaving only the name, Puerta de Tierra, for a wide blighted area. The largest section was called, with folk simplicity, Sal Si Puedes . . . Get Out If You Can. The houses of Sal Si Puedes, made of scraps of wood, cardboard, and thatch, rose on stilts above a stagnant mud flat. A walkway of rubber tires connected them to dry ground.

There were other slums flung out across the city. El Fanguito, the Little Mudhole . . . Buena Vista, a miasmal swamp . . . La Colectora, where pestilent waters collected and fever-bearing mosquitoes bred. Farther out there were Behind-the-Roundhouse and the sinister alleys of The Zone of Seven Daggers.

On the muddy streets of these outcast communities, Felisa Rincón now set her dainty feet. Like most members of the Popular Party, who were doctors and lawyers and teachers and engineers rather than politicians, Felisa had never pictured herself speaking to a crowd on a street corner. She flinched at the thought. Not being an orator, she began just to talk to people, telling them about the ideals of the Popular Party and what it could do if they would believe in it and support it. She had no political phrases or mannerisms. She was just a woman explaining something she believed in deeply and sincerely herself. Her message got across.

Sometimes, the Populars went out in numbers with a sound truck and banners. At other times, there was just Felisa, alone, talking to the people in house after house about their lives and their problems and what could be done about them.

She spent less and less time in her Style Shop. While she was there, fitting a creation for some wealthy lady, a knot of poor women would gather outside, waiting for her to finish. She had made appointments to take them to the hospital, to help their sons get jobs or, perhaps, to take their children to buy shoes. Her own family having grown up, she now adopted the great family of the poor and lavished her love and energy on them.

The slum dwellers, looking up from their misery at the beautiful woman stepping toward them across the mud, were daring to believe that the Popular Party might help them. Like the *jíbaro* who first saw her in her white ball gown, they began to say, "She is an angel, a saint, the Virgin Mary come to redeem us!"

Felisa's Style Shop, in the end, closed its doors because the proprietress had no time to put into it. The other Populars, too, were neglecting their professions to put longer and longer hours into their crusade.

Sometimes, they would meet in the Rincóns' house in Luna Street to plan strategy. Afterwards, there would be refreshments, prepared by the chairman of the Municipal Committee. Then guitars would come out and they would sing.

The songs summed up their feelings and aspirations. "Jalda Arriba" . . . "Up the Hill" . . . was their anthem. Another that ran through their lives like a theme was "Borinquén Lament" (Borinquén being an old Indian name for the island).

Rafael Hernández, the Puerto Rican composer who had written the song, had himself lived for years in Sal Si Puedes. Through the gift of music, he was one of the few who did get out, but, from the scars on his memory, he wrote of a little *jíbaro* who comes to town

Doña Felisa

to sell his small crop only to find the market dead and deserted and no one with money to buy.

The song is usually called "El Jibarito"—"The Little *Jíbaro*." Wandering through the town strangled by poverty, *El Jibarito* laments . . .

> Borinquén, land of Eden,
> That the great poet Gautier called
> The pearl of the seas . . .
> Now, you are dying of your sorrows.
> The lament is heard
> Everywhere on my poor island.
> What will become of Puerto Rico, my dear God?
> What will become of my children?
> And my home?

Felisa's clear voice was like a waving banner when she sang "Jalda Arriba." But when she sang "El Jibarito," the tears ran down her face.

CHAPTER

VIII

———◆———

A Sword and a Rose

IT WAS early on New Year's Eve when Samuel Quiñones headed downtown to buy a present for his fiancée, Clara. Quiñones was Don Enrique's young law partner and a hard-working Popular. He brought his friend, Genaro Gautier, along for company—a tall, lanky lawyer from Ponce who was the new Popular Party's secretary for San Juan.

Before they reached the store, the two young politicos met two young lady politicos, the Rincón sisters. The four having so much in common, it was a pleasant meeting.

Fini reminded Sam that she was now selling perfumes in her spare time, to make some money, and he bought some for Clara. Then the girls invited the men home to join a few of their friends for New Year's Eve. Sam had to get back to his fiancée, but Genaro accepted with pleasure.

Home to the corner of Cruz and Luna they walked,

47

through the narrow, blue brick streets with the balconies overhead. Genaro's tall, lean build, intensely blue eyes, and keen mind made an impression on Felisa from the beginning. Related to the famous nineteenth-century poet, José Gautier Benítez, Genaro was deeply schooled in literature. He could recite from his famous relative's works and declaimed with gusto Gautier's famous poem, "To Puerto Rico."

> In vain, my homeland, I draw my breath far from you.
> Always, always, I see you with the eyes of my soul.
> You gave life to the one I love.
> I love her because of you
> And I love you because of her.

As the evening advanced, Genaro quoted other poems with less emphasis on the homeland. When he had Felisa's ear alone, he even quoted some verses of his own, although it was hard to have a private conversation in that lively household.

There was singing, of course. Felisa and Genaro blended their voices for a while. Then they repaired to a corner where she showed him her collection of Spanish fans and, with sparkle-eyed demonstrations, taught him the romantic language of the fan.

To open and close quickly means "I am not interested. Go away!" To snap the fan closed means "Be careful, Mama is watching!" Or Papa? To kiss the top of the fan means "I love you!"

Genaro had thought to pick up a bottle of champagne on the way to the house. At midnight, the couple

A Sword and a Rose

toasted, looking into each other's eyes as the New Year came in. When he finally left, he had an invitation to return for New Year's lunch, now only a matter of hours away.

Felisa, strangely exhilarated, stayed up to straighten the house a little, after everyone was gone. Finding the cork from Genaro's champagne bottle, she held it close in her hand for a while, then tucked it in her drawer for a souvenir. She would have it for a long, long time.

"She is like Bolívar," poet Llorens Torres said about Felisa. "She comes with a sword in one hand and a rose in the other and uses whichever one seems appropriate!"

Felisa was a tough fighter for what she believed was right. In the party councils, she could be a stubborn exponent for a point of view, adamant in argument, but just as often she could win her point with smiles and soft words. When all else failed, sometimes she even fell back on feminine tears to persuade a tough colleague. Her fellow Populars marveled at her and sometimes compared her to Queen Isabella, Mother of the New World, who combined the gentleness of a woman with the strength of spirit of a man.

From New Year's Day on, in 1939, Felisa had a companion in her work who was as dedicated as she to the party's goals, one who, like her, put his personal life second to the cause. They were a team. Felisa, talking, persuading, making friends . . . Genaro keeping track of voters and locations, piling up a ward by ward voting register to make party work more effective.

They walked together through Danger Street in Sal Si Puedes and he held her hand, helping her across the bridge of rubber tires. In La Perla, as other young couples plan "Here we will put the sofa . . . there we will put the chair," Felisa and Genaro looked at the horrid hillside and said, "Here we will put pavement . . . there a street light . . . and where the slaughterhouse is now, we will put a Community Center instead!"

They made many friends. They were invited to weddings, following gay bridal parties to the pathetic little slum church. Sometimes, they walked with a funeral procession through narrow alleys to the ancient cemetery of Santa María de la Magdalena de Pazzis on the hillside between La Perla and the great gray bulk of El Morro Fortress.

They would linger, sadly, after a funeral, wandering among the bleached monuments that held so much of the history of their city. Around the domed pantheon in the center, the graves were closed-packed, for San Juaners had been brought to rest there for a hundred years. All around were the passionate messages of the bereft. They lingered under the gaze of a marble angel to read,

> I was loved.
> I loved.
> The sun shone on me.
> Life, you owe me nothing.
> Life, we are at peace.

A Sword and a Rose

Antonio Barceló, the old Liberal leader had died recently and was buried there. So were José de Diego, the great poet-patriot of the previous generation, and Gautier Benítez, Genaro's famous ancestor. A tall shaft rose to Gautier's memory with a bust of the bearded poet and, carved in marble, his last poem, asking to be buried in "this beloved Puerto Rican earth."

Supervising the campaign in the whole city, Felisa and Genaro took personal charge of La Perla and passed most of the hours of the day there. Picking their way up the hill in the darkness of night, they would watch the great tropical stars appear over the ancient city walls and, hand in hand, they would speculate on how many votes they had won that day.

IX

———◆———

"Last of the Gentlemen"

DON ENRIQUE RINCÓN, who had looked favorably on very few of Felisa's admirers, found much in common with Genaro Gautier. Both men came from fine old families. Both were cultivated, knew literature, and endeavored to create it. Both were convivial with men but traditional in their ideas about women.

As Genaro's visits became more frequent, Don Enrique was not displeased.

"Genaro," he said. "You are one of the last of the gentlemen!"

Genaro, like Felisa, had not married at the conventional early age. Friends said he would never marry. He liked his freedom and his late hours too much, they said. But Genaro's friends were wrong.

In March of 1939, he and Felisa drew up a guest list for their wedding. When they looked at it, they were horrified. To plan for such a colossal social event when they were campaigning day and night would be impossible. They decided to go very quietly to Trujillo Alto and be married in the old church where Felisa's mother and father had married.

According to church custom, the wedding should have taken place in the bride's parish, in San Juan Cathedral. To marry elsewhere required special waivers. When the bride, in a wedding dress of her own design, and the groom, in white flannels and blue serge coat, arrived at the church, the priest informed them that their waivers were not in order.

They had taken a day off—one day. The election was a matter of just months away now. Judges were sitting half the night registering prospective voters. Felisa's territory was the island's largest population center. Thousands of signatures were still needed and activity was at fever pitch. They had to be back in the front lines the next day.

But the priest was handing back their documents. He regretted, but . . .

It was too much for Felisa. For a moment, the party leader replaced the bride.

"Father," she said, "marry us! If you have to bend the rules, do it. But we must get married today. There is no other time."

The priest hesitated, then took back the documents and proceeded with the wedding.

The day was the Feast of Salvador Gloria. The church was full of calla lilies. As a row of saints carved long ago by Spanish artisans looked on, Felisa Rincón became Felisa Rincón de Gautier.

The newlyweds drove back to town to a small family party. The next day, they were back in the slums, campaigning.

Since they started work so early and stayed so late, there would be no time to find and furnish a home before the elections. Instead, the Gautiers moved a bed down to their office and kept on with their grueling schedule.

Election Day required a final burst of energy. Was there fraud reported in one district? Intimidation of voters in another? The chairman of the Municipal Committee had to be every place at once.

Along with the physical strain there was the gnawing worry about what the poor would do, now that the time of reckoning was here. They had been deceived so many times in the past. Would they believe the Populars' promises? Or would hunger win out, making them take the two dollars and vote the same old way?

When the polls closed, Felisa hurried to the crowded room that was their home to freshen up before going to wait for the returns. She put on a good dress and her pearl earrings and tucked some jasmine in her hair, prepared to meet either victory or defeat in style.

Before leaving, she paused, thinking, "Just one minute to pray."

She sat down in a chair, clasped her hands, closed her eyes and began, "Oh God, give us light . . ." That was as far as she got. She had not slept in three days and now, suddenly, she sank into oblivion.

Through the night, trucks of ballots were arriving in San Juan from all parts of the island, each with a caravan of vote-watchers' cars following it. The trucks lumbered to the capital where the ballots were unloaded and the count verified.

At headquarters, the Populars received the results with growing joy. Felisa, upright in her chair at home, slept on.

When she woke the next morning, Genaro was there to tell her the news. It was victory. The Populars had won the election.

After the election, Felisa and Genaro went to El Yunque, the tropical rain forest, not far from San Juan for a honeymoon. They ended it with a visit to Yabucoa, where both had grandparents.

"Let me tell you about your grandfathers," Genaro's grandmother, ninety years old, said. "They knew each other well in this town. Felisa, your grandfather was a pharmacist and Mayor of Yabucoa. He was a devout church-goer and very, very conservative in politics. He started the Conservative Party Club here.

"Genaro's grandfather was also a pharmacist, and he became the Mayor of Ponce. He never went to church and was a strong liberal. He started the Liberal Party Club here."

Doña Felisa

The old lady raised her eyes toward heaven. "Oh, how those two *caballeros* hated each other!" she said. "If they could come alive again and hear about your marriage, they would both die again—of shock!"

X

The First Alcaldesa

"WILL YOU accept appointment as Mayor of San Juan?"

Felisa had known this was coming. She took a deep breath.

"No," she said.

"You would be the first *Alcaldesa* in our history!" (An *Alcaldesa* is a lady Mayor.)

"No," Felisa said.

She had two reasons for refusing. Her father and her husband. They knew the Mayor was leaving office and that the Party wanted to appoint Felisa to finish his term, but both men objected strenuously.

Commitee work? All right. Holding public office? Never!

From years of habit, she still bowed to the will of the men in the family. When Genaro wanted her to cut her long hair, she had cried but cut it. She had two thick braids made from the hair and wore them in a halo around her head, so the loss was not total.

Doña Felisa

But as for being Mayor—all she could do was put the idea resolutely out of her mind.

On September 28, 1945, the sun set in a blood-red sky. Islanders know that sign. They hardly need the confirmation of the warning flags hung out by the Weather Bureau.

The next morning, a hard rain was falling and everyone prepared for a hurricane.

Felisa and Genaro had a big house in Old San Juan and the slum dwellers whom she had helped so often before began knocking on her door, asking to bring their children in for safety. She knew that every bad storm washed away scores of shacks along the shore. They were found floating far out at sea, later, often with the people still inside, drowned. Felisa opened her doors.

By noon, she had three hundred guests, and babies were beginning to cry for lunch. The *rafagos* were blowing—erratic gusts that precede the main storm—when she set out to get help. She went to the Governor, the Mayor, Civil Defense, the Red Cross. All said they would be glad to give help—as soon as the storm was over. When she got home, there were four hundred people bulging out of her house.

Felisa asked several men to accompany her and went to the public school which was locked up for the week end.

"I'll take the responsibility," she said. "Kick down the doors!"

The First Alcaldesa

She went back and led her hundreds through the storm to the school.

Fighting her way through increasing wind and rain, she went to the grocery store and bought $250 worth of food. "Put it on my charge account," she said. Back at the school, she fed over a thousand people and then started games for the children and community singing.

After the hurricane, Felisa had made up her mind.

"If I'm going to have the responsibility," she said, "I might as well have the authority, so I can do things right!"

Genaro was resigned when he heard the news that she would accept appointment as Mayor. He had come to realize that his wife was a unique person in politics. There was no one else like her in her relationship with the people of San Juan. It might as well be made official.

Don Enrique definitely was not resigned to the idea. He took the news of her appointment hard. But Felisa was following her destiny now and he had, in the end, to accept it.

On December 23, there was a party to celebrate the appointment of the new Mayor. It was a time of double joy for Felisa—her appointment and the arrival of Christmas, the Rincóns' most important day together. She was to go to the celebration in the company of the retiring Mayor, so Genaro and Don Enrique went together.

The party was at the Guadalquivir Club, a restaurant overlooking the ocean, open to the breezes on three sides. A lively orchestra was playing as Genaro and Enrique entered. Genaro saw a nephew of Enrique, Dr. José Correa, and stopped to talk. Enrique, tall and distinguished in immaculate whites, asked a young lady to dance.

As they whirled across the floor, suddenly he stopped. "I feel dizzy," he said. "Let's sit down."

Then he crumpled to the floor.

The dancers rushed to his side. Genaro and Dr. Correa pushed quickly through the crowd. A nurse, one of the guests, was already kneeling beside him. As the doctor joined her, she said, "His breath has stopped."

The doctor paused, then he said slowly, "His life has stopped."

"An ambulance! Quick! We must get him to a hospital." It was Felisa crying out.

"Felisa," the doctor said, "it's too late."

"Impossible," she said. "I don't believe it! Get an ambulance!"

"Felisa . . ." the doctor started. Then he sighed and signaled a friend to get an ambulance.

The crowd stood silent, accepting the truth. But the first *Alcaldesa* of San Juan knelt beside her father, saying over and over again, "No. No. I don't believe it."

XI

---•—•—

"A Job of Housekeeping"

FELISA AND Fini shuddered as a rat scuttled out of the shadows then back into them again. Felisa bent to pick up a paper off the floor. It was handwritten in a florid antique penmanship.

"Acts of the City Council of San Juan Bautista . . . 18 September 1753 . . ."

When the new Mayor moved in, the old City Hall was in a state of decay. It had a right to be. Parts of it dated from the 1600's. Deep in the dusty storerooms, the old Spanish archives still lay, yellowed, curling, and besieged by termites.

Even the twentieth-century parts of the building were in disrepair. Felisa didn't know whether to begin on the littered terrace on the top floor or in the rat-infested basement. In the end, she went to work everywhere at once. She appointed Fini as Municipal Secretary. One of her duties would be to organize and preserve the historical archives. Meanwhile, a committee of government officials' wives would work on the building itself, bringing the high-ceilinged ancient rooms back to a state of dignity again.

Beyond the walls of the City Hall, the real job was waiting. San Juan had suffered years of neglect under both Spaniards and Americans. At the turn of the century, political prisoners were sometimes sentenced to clean up the garbage in the city streets. It was an excellent revenge, but a poor system of sanitation. When Felisa took office, the city owned no more than eight open garbage trucks. Now, she set out to get new ones. The City Council did not care to go overboard on that type of expenditure, but Felisa was eloquent as never before. She was fiery and passionate! She refused to take no for an answer. When they gave her a few, she came back for more. As she had once cherished her collection of Spanish fans, she now began to take pride in her fleet of immaculate modern garbage trucks.

One of Felisa's first acts was to keep her promise to the people of La Perla. The slaughterhouse came down. After years of degradation, suddenly La Perlans were breathing the clean trade wind that the rest of the island enjoyed. Where the slaughterhouse had stood a Community Center went up.

The ragged people waiting on line with their buckets at the City Hall water tap were seen no more. Felisa arranged for clean water to run directly to each slum area. Pavement on the streets that had run with mud, street

"A Job of Housekeeping"

lights, and ambulance service brought the slum dwellers into the fold of civilization, at last.

The poor were the majority in San Juan when Felisa Rincón took office and she gave them all she could. But she did more than give to them. She inspired them with hope and pride and the spirit to do for themselves. She urged them to repair their shacks, to visit the new government clinics, to get their children to school every day.

There were those, of the old Spanish traditions, who were shocked at the idea of giving a woman the job of Mayor. When she was criticized, Felisa didn't get angry. She looked her critics in the eye and said, "Do you have any ideas for doing this better?"

If good suggestions were forthcoming, she adopted them. When people complimented her on the improved conditions in the city, she smiled modestly.

"It's a job of housekeeping," she said.

XII

———◆●◆———

"Love, Not Politics..."

RAFAEL HERNÁNDEZ, the song writer who had grown up in Sal Si Puedes, was rewriting "El Jibarito" with a happy ending.

It was a sign of the times.

Perhaps the *jíbaros* were not entirely out of their difficulties, but things were changing and changing fast on the island. The Popular Party was keeping its promises to the people. Its social laws had been passed. Fifty thousand landless peasants had been given small farms of their own. Many of the others had found jobs in industry, for the government program called Operation Bootstrap was inducing manufacturers to start more and more plants on the island.

New schools, hospitals, reservoirs were being built and the world's largest low-cost housing project was helping to reduce the number of slum dwellings.

The old fight over status came up from time to time, but Muñoz Marín had introduced a new concept in

Felisa receives the Order of the Holy Sepulcher of Jerusalem from Cardinal Spell-
man in St. Patrick's Cathedral, New York City

A gift of roses from Manhattan
Boy Scouts

Puerto Rico Information Service

Below: A moment at Doña
Felisa's trial

Archivo El Mundo

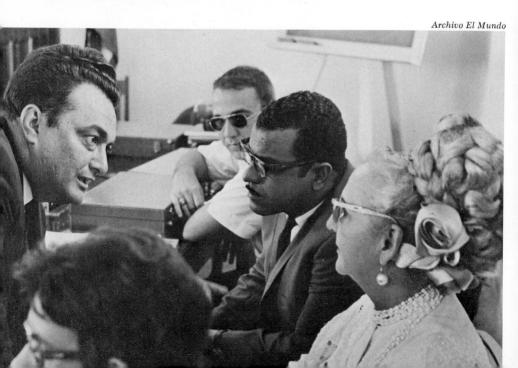

Felisa rides a sled in the snow

Below: Snowball fight in San Juan. The Mayor is at right.

The poster reads "With Muñoz and Felisa to the Top of the Hill!"

The home Felisa built for "her retirement" in the suburb of Caimito

Felisa with her niece and
Director of Public Relations,
Cuchi Rincón de Rubiano

Archivo El Mundo

At the Festival Casals, Felisa enjoys the company of sister Fini (left), and niece
Ketty Palerm, Municipal Secretary.

Archivo El Mundo

View of El Fanguito from the bridge

La Perla after a *marejada*

Walking with a friend in La Perla

Left: Doña Felisa on her seventy-first birthday. *Below:* The Mayor's birthday.

American politics and won for the island the status of Commonwealth. Puerto Rico was now a free state, self-governed, while retaining its ties with the United States.

After Felisa's term of appointment expired, she was elected by a landslide. She continued to be elected by a big majority every four years.

Her fleet of garbage trucks now numbered 140. San Juan was a clean city. Hotels had blossomed on the beaches and tourists were flocking to them. Felisa widened streets, restored old buildings, sponsored cultural events, and pioneered in public nursery schools.

Clearing the slums was an uphill job, because of the Puerto Rican birth rate. It was one of the highest in the world. As the new housing projects went up, so did the population. But gradually the slums were shrinking inwards. Sal Si Puedes disappeared. Behind-the-Roundhouse and The Zone of Seven Daggers were only ugly memories. At Buena Vista, the people who had been living in a swamp began to fill it in themselves. The city helped with trucks of fill whenever it could. Over the years, the people of Buena Vista gradually got rid of the stilts on their houses and lived on solid ground made with their own labor.

The official residence of the Mayor of San Juan was a charming villa on the outskirts of town. It was quiet, beautiful, with a garden full of *reinitas,* Puerto Rico's tiny, typical, black and yellow birds. In the morning rush hour, the Mayor's limousine could reach City Hall

Doña Felisa

in forty minutes. Felisa tried it for a few months. Then she added up the time she had spent traveling.

"I need those hours," she said, and she and Genaro moved into a few small rooms on the top floor of City Hall. There was just enough room in the bedroom for a bed, a small table, and the shrines of her saints.

They were there, always, on the wall and the table, for religion never left Felisa's life. Our Lady of Perpetual Help, the Sacred Heart of Jesus, the dark-skinned Virgin of Guadalupe, our Lady of Providence—the statues stood, plaster, carved wood, hammered silver, each with a candle or a few flowers before it. Many times in her busy days, she stopped before them to pray.

She needed the solace of her shrines often in her personal life, for the Rincóns had more than their share of family problems. Her brother, Enrique, died young of a heart attack. Moncho died after two tragic months of illness in which Felisa visited him almost every day, going on to perform her municipal duties with a breaking heart. Fini's health forced her to curtail her activities in public life.

Genaro's health, too, was poor. He worked for the Department of Justice for a while and later did legal research at the Capitol, but he was not able to throw himself into political life as he had in the past. He had two heart attacks—one more gnawing worry in Felisa's heart. But he still acted as Felisa's campaign manager.

"We are always young and healthy at campaign time," he said.

"Love, Not Politics . . ."

Genaro was a gentle spirit who never begrudged his wife the limelight. When the Prince Consort of Holland visited San Juan, Felisa and Genaro entertained him at City Hall. Genaro smiled later. "I, too, know what it is to be Prince Consort," he said.

Her large family left Felisa open to many sorrows—but of course it also brought her many joys as a troop of nieces and nephews grew up around her. In the old Puerto Rican family tradition, she often found them jobs close to her in the government.

Felisa's political opponents never let her forget that the City Hall was full of Rincóns. Her cousin, María Alvarez, became her executive aide. Cuchi, her niece, was her Director of Public Relations. Her niece, Cuca Saldaña, was head of the Diagnostic Clinic. When Fini went to New York to live, niece Ketty Palerm took over the job of Municipal Secretary.

Each of these young women was keen and qualified but—so many nieces! Felisa had a quick response to that criticism.

"I wish I had a dozen more nieces," she said. "They work harder for less money."

If she brought her family into the government, Felisa also made thousands of citizens feel like they were part of her family.

"She hugs people just to get votes!" unsuccessful candidates from other parties cried. Indeed, when she inspected a school, she hugged the children. When she went through a slum, she hugged old people and cried over their troubles with them. She was a mother to all San Juan. But the affection did not wane after an election. It continued unabated all the days of all the years.

Felisa herself once summed up her philosophy in a press interview.

"Love, not politics, is what gets things done."

XIII

—◆—

Wednesday Morning

BEARDED AND mustachioed, a row of paintings of former Mayors of San Juan looked down at the crowd hurrying in to fill the room where once they received visiting dignitaries. Now, on Wednesdays, the visiting dignitaries are the poor, for that day is the day of Doña Felisa's Open House.

The rows of wooden chairs are filled. There are white faces and black, and faces with high, Indian cheekbones. All are turned toward the white-haired, turbaned lady sitting in front of the room at a big, glass-topped table. The lady is writing on a memo pad.

A young man sits down at her table. He shows her photographs. He explains his problem passionately. He is engaged to a Dominican girl and can't get her into the country. It is just a technicality, but he can't afford a lawyer to remedy it.

Felisa beckons to a legal aide and they put their heads together. The legal aide walks out with the young man.

Doña Felisa

"I am blind. Blind! They are tearing down my building! What is to become of me?" An old lady cries and wrings her hands.

Felisa is firm. "Calm yourself! Calm yourself! Going to pieces will not do any good!"

She confers with an aide, then scribbles a note to the Housing Department. The old lady leans over her chair and hugs her. Felisa hugs the old lady in return.

One person after another sits down opposite the Mayor. She talks to each one, smiles, furrows her brow, then writes a note and tears it off her pad. She has many sharpened pencils on her table.

A harried, toil-worn woman comes up with two toddlers. She has seven more children at home. She cannot make ends meet. Her husband makes twenty dollars a week, so they are not eligible for welfare. Mrs. Iglesias, a City Hall social worker, comes forward for a murmured conference. The woman will get a weekly food note. Also, the two oldest children have outgrown their shoes. They are barefoot. The long pencil makes another note. "Two pairs."

The San Juan poor receive welfare funds from the United States and Puerto Rican governments. But there are so many poor that the funds don't stretch far enough. The city has a fund of a few thousand dollars for these small emergencies. Sometimes the money runs out early. Felisa's aide looks at the note for eyeglasses or boards to fix a leaky roof or food money for someone who is hungry.

Wednesday Morning

"It's gone, Doña Felisa. We've used up the money for this month."

Felisa doesn't grasp the kind of mathematics that says a hungry person can't eat till next month.

"This woman is hungry," she says. "Find the money somewhere!"

The other political parties take a dim view of her unorthodox financing. But the hungry find her methods logical.

Lunch time comes and goes and she is still at her table.

"They know I will never leave while anyone is sitting here with a problem," she says. "That's the value of Open House. The poorest person knows he matters here.

"It's valuable to me, too. If there is something wrong in this city, it comes to my attention. If there's a problem in the schools or a bad hole in the street, I hear about it. If there's a crooked official, anyone can come here and complain."

It is after two before the last person has talked to her and left.

Felisa takes the elevator up to her apartment on the fifth floor. She looks at her watch. "I have ten minutes before the Council meeting. Just time enough to finish that hem."

Genaro's niece is getting married. Felisa walks into the next room where a dressmaker's dummy stands in a white lace wedding dress. The Mayor of San Juan, her mouth full of pins, kneels down on the floor to work.

71

XIV

———◆———

"I Warn You..."

"*Viva! Viva,* Doña Felisa!"

It was Governor Rockefeller, leaning from the review-ing stand to wave to her. The Mayor of San Juan waved back from her open car in the Puerto Rican Day parade and blew kisses to the Governor of New York.

From the beginning, Felisa came to the States often, for celebrations, to receive honorary degrees, and to campaign.

"Don't campaign in New York," her advisors had al-ways told her. "Down here, you and your party are win-ners. Up there, who knows how things come out? Don't take a chance on campaigning for a loser."

"You have to be loyal to your friends," Felisa main-tained. "There are 800,000 Puerto Ricans in New York. If anyone is trying to help them, I'll campaign for him, win or lose."

She held to her principles and continued to campaign in New York. As the Puerto Rican migrants traveled across the country, she did, too—to Chicago, Philadelphia, Miami—all the major American cities. The smiling face, the turban and earrings became familiar on American television.

American magazines and newspapers marveled at this fantastic lady from the Caribbean. "She combines the grandeur of a Spanish *marquesa* with the bumptious energy of Fiorello La Guardia," said *Life* magazine. *Harper's Bazaar* voted her one of the world's outstanding women.

"My English is so bad," she would say modestly. But it wasn't, and she won as many friends among the native Americans as among the Puerto Ricans.

Language was never a barrier to Felisa. "She speaks the language of humanity," her friends say.

They recall her in Tokyo Airport, trying to talk to a distinguished Japanese gentleman who happened to be sitting near her. He did not understand Spanish or English but when she spoke to him he jumped up and bowed graciously. Here was something both understood, so Felisa rose and joined him in bowing. With the aid of sign language, they exchanged names, and bowed again and smiled at each other. As they moved off to separate planes, they were still bowing happily.

In Hong Kong, Felisa shocked her hosts by asking to visit the slums. "I don't go to criticize," she explained, "but to get to know the people."

Reluctantly, they took her to the terrible hillside where the refugees from Red China camped.

Doña Felisa

"It is full of disease," she was warned. "Don't shake any hands! Don't eat anything!"

But she had to be herself. She walked into the shacks where ten people lived in one room and hugged the children and stroked their matted hair and drank the tea their mothers offered, while her aides nervously planned to wash her in alcohol when they got home.

Always she wanted to meet the people. Not just the officials—the people.

In one South American country, she was touring a town whose population was Indian. She expressed a desire to get acquainted with some of them.

Her highly-placed host expressed regrets. "I warn you about these Indians, Doña Felisa," he said. "They are not friendly to white people. They are, in fact, hostile. It is very difficult to communicate with them."

Felisa greeted a young Indian girl. As her host had predicted, the girl ignored her. But Felisa wasn't discouraged.

"How pretty you are!" she said.

The girl stole a sideways glance.

"Do you have a boyfriend?"

The girl couldn't help smiling.

Doña Felisa kept talking, asking questions, admiring. At last, a woman approached her with a cup.

"Don't drink!" her host said hastily. "This native drink is . . ." He shuddered expressively.

But Felisa was already drinking it. *"Mil gracias!"* she smiled. "A thousand thanks! How delicious!"

"I Warn You . . ."

In a few minutes a crowd of Indians had gathered around Doña Felisa, asking and answering questions.

"If only everyone could travel. Then people could understand each other," Felisa always said.

One thing that made her sad when she traveled north was the sight of snow. "If only our tropical children could see the snow. If only they could have the fun of making snowballs, just once!"

When she met Captain Eddie Rickenbacker, president of Eastern Airlines, she said the same thing to him. One March day, Captain Rickenbacker sent two special insulated bags to New Hampshire. Local children were standing by with shovels to fill them with newly fallen snow. The bags, each one holding a ton of snow, sped by truck to Boston Airport where they were loaded onto an Eastern Constellation and flown over 2,000 miles of ocean to San Juan.

The Mayor met the plane at the airport. With a motorcycle escort, the snow sped to Muñoz Rivera Park. Thousands of waiting children greeted it with screams of delight.

The scene that took place then was something new under the Puerto Rican sun. Doña Felisa Rincón threw the first snowball and then it was a free-for-all. The joy of snow-down-the-neck came for the first time to thousands. They put up a slide and Felisa took her turn going down it on a sled. A snowman rose, to the wild cheers of the crowd. The snow from New Hampshire lasted for thirty glorious minutes.

Felisa had provided several truckloads of oranges as refreshments for the children. As the snow melted, the happy crowd turned to the oranges and threw them instead of snowballs in a hilarious continuation of the fun. When everyone was thoroughly sticky, the youngsters ate their oranges and began to drift home.

As the Mayor's party left, Felisa looked around at the clean, tree-lined streets and neat buildings.

"How different," she said wistfully, "from when Sal Si Puedes was here!"

XV

———————

"Without a Good Friday..."

"PRAISE HIM . . . praise Him . . . praise Him . . ."

The towering silver monstrance sways on its platform as the faithful carry it down the narrow street. The red robes of the Bishop trail on the blue bricks. The procession winds through the streets of the Old City as it has on the day of Corpus Christi since the first streets were laid down in San Juan in the 1500's. It is a sober day of worship for Catholics.

It is night and the torches burn high. Rich and poor mingle in the flickering light as they follow the chanting nuns. In the marching crowd is a white-haired lady in a turban and dangling earrings. The Mayor of San Juan joins her fellow Catholics on foot behind the holy relics of the Cathedral.

"Praise the Lord . . . praise the Lord . . . praise the Lord . . ."

Because she was an ardent Catholic, naturally Felisa was asked to speak at the big rally in favor of religious teaching in the schools. Forty thousand people attended the rally and roared approval of the speakers.

It was an impressive demonstration. If only, some of its sponsors thought, if only this religious fervor could be channeled into a political party. Not only could they win religious education in the schools, but they could challenge the government's policy of giving out birth control information in public health clinics. It was a tempting idea.

Shortly after the great rally, the Christian Action Party was born. The Popular Party, with its record of big majorities, did not worry much about the new party—until September 3, 1960, two months before the election. Then the blow fell.

Puerto Ricans across the island were fanning themselves at Sunday morning Mass when their priests departed from the Latin ritual to read a letter. It was a pastoral letter from the Bishops of Puerto Rico. Its message was simple. Certain policies of the Popular Party—obviously those regarding religious education and birth control—were contrary to the teachings of the Church. The philosophy of the Popular Party was therefore anti-Church and anti-Catholic. Anyone who voted for the Popular Party would be excommunicated.

Religion was half Felisa's life. The Popular Party was the other half. She was shaken by the cruel decree that threatened to take one or the other away from her.

"I will not resign from the Popular Party," she said.

She went as usual to Mass on Sunday, prayed as usual

and, as usual, walked slowly toward the altar for Communion.

The priest came down the line of communicants with the Holy Eucharist, offering it to each in turn. The man beside Felisa took it. The priest blessed him. Then he walked past the kneeling Mayor of San Juan without looking at her and began to administer the Sacrament to the woman on the other side.

Felisa Rincón left the church with tears in her eyes.

In the coming months, for the first time in her life, she was denied the comfort of Communion and confession.

"I will not resign from the Popular Party," she said. "The Bishop is against me. But God is above the Bishop and I believe that God is with me."

Over Puerto Rican rooftops, among the *jíbaro* flags of the Popular Party, the rosary flag of the Christian Action Party began to appear.

Muñoz Marín, running for re-election as Governor, refused to fight the Church. "I am not running for Bishop because I don't know anything about the job," he said. "And the Bishop should not run for my job.

"Continue being a religious person," he told the crowds at his rallies. "Have God on your side. But don't let the Bishop tell you how to vote."

On Election Day, with the threat of excommunication over the whole electorate, Puerto Ricans voted overwhelmingly to re-elect Muñoz Marín, Felisa Rincón, and all the Popular Party candidates. Out of seventy-seven townships, they won seventy-six.

Doña Felisa

The Sunday after the election, Felisa went to Mass as usual. Was she to be excommunicated? It was time to find out.

She walked slowly up to the altar where the congregation was receiving Communion. She knelt down.

The priest offered her the wafer. When she had taken it, he made the sign of the cross over her and blessed her.

Thousands of other Puerto Ricans went to church with sinking hearts that Sunday and received with relief like Felisa's the blessing of the Church. No one was excommunicated.

For a long time, Felisa kept a letter she had received, in the dark days, from a nun of the order of Notre Dame —a nun who also sympathized with the Popular Party.

"Doña Felisa," it read, "never forget that without a Good Friday there could be no Resurrection Sunday."

XVI

———◆———

"What You Must Pay"

DOÑA FELISA looked at the trophies and plaques on the wall of her small room.

"With profound gratitude from 10,000 Camp Fire Girls who enjoyed the richness of your hospitality at the Horizon Club Conference Afloat."

"With the thanks of the National Postal Union . . ."

"The Altruism Award for Extraordinary Dedication to the Philosophy of Unselfishness . . ."

"Woman of the Americas—1954"

Her face was blank as she slowly wound her familiar turban. She was going on trial for misuse of public funds.

The Commonwealth government was proud of its reputation for honesty. The absence of corruption in Puerto Rico had been noted with admiration by international observers. Politicians did not get rich on the island. One thing that kept it that way was the scrupulous auditing system.

Doña Felisa

Officials all over the island had their records audited annually by the government. Every penny had to be accounted for. Once in a while, the Mayor of some town was brought up on charges, but there had been no real scandals.

That's why the news exploded like a bombshell when the auditor announced the charges against the Mayor of San Juan—misuse of public funds.

"She is no different from the others," he was quoted as saying. "The irregularities are there. She must answer." Politically, the auditor was not a follower of Doña Felisa.

Her fellow officials in the Department of Justice flinched, reading the charges. But the clean-government machinery was inexorable. They prepared to prosecute her.

In San Juan's City Hall, all work ceased. People were stunned. It couldn't have happened. Not that they believed Doña Felisa had done anything wrong. No one who knew her even considered the possibility. It was the enormity of bothering her with unjust accusations that upset them.

She sat stony-faced in court as the charges were read. A sum of money had been appropriated for public works. She had dipped into that money for the benefit of private persons.

The prosecution produced a witness to prove its case.

"What You Must Pay"

The witness was a woman from La Perla. She cried because she had to testify against Doña Felisa.

The charge, when boiled down, was this: The sum of money had been appropriated for improvements in La Perla. Improvements had been made in the streets. That was all right. Work had been done on the Community Center. That was all right. But there had been a few dollars left over from the project. An old lady who lived near the Community Center had had her roof damaged in a storm. Noticing it, Doña Felisa had ordered that the left over dollars be used to repair the roof. The old lady, on the witness stand, weepingly admitted it had been done. But why, oh why, was it wrong? she wanted to know.

Felisa's lawyers rose and said that it was not wrong, that money appropriated for improvements in La Perla could indeed be used for a private house. They cited section and paragraph in the law to prove their point.

The charges were dismissed.

There were other charges. The law required that construction of public works must be given out for bids from private construction companies. Doña Felisa had ignored that law and had the city do a certain job itself, with its own equipment.

Her lawyers replied again. Yes, new public works had to be offered for bids. But improvements in previously completed public works did not. The work in question was the making of a parking lot on the center safety island of a city boulevard. The parking lot (for students at a nearby school) was not a new public work, Felisa's lawyers pointed out. It was an improvement on the already existing safety island and therefore not required to be offered for bids.

The charges were dismissed.

Felisa sat grimly through the days as one charge after another was brought up and dismissed. There was no suggestion that she had profited or used any city money dishonestly. There was only a series of technicalities, the result of the long-suppressed dissatisfaction of the technically-minded with her "meet the people's needs first, then look up the rules" financial methods. At last, she was exonerated of all accusation of misuse of funds.

Back in her apartment, slowly unwinding her turban, she looked again at the plaques on her wall.

"Felisa Rincón de Gautier . . . One of the 100 Outstanding Women of the World . . ."

"Awarded to Felisa Rincón de Gautier by the New Jersey Conference of Mayors for outstanding and meritorious service in the advancement of good government."

"If anyone had told me," Felisa said to the silent friends who stood by, "if anyone had told me what you must pay to serve the public, I would never have believed it!"

XVII

—●—

"Las Mañanitas"

Wake up, my dear, awaken.
Look—the light of dawn!
Listen—birds are singing!
The moon's already gone.

The serenaders were schoolchildren. They stood on
the fifth-floor terrace of City Hall at six o'clock in the
morning, singing "Las Mañanitas," the Spanish birthday
greeting.

Doña Felisa woke up and remembered that she was
seventy years old.

The birthday party was held in the plaza in front of
the Cathedral, under the shiny green umbrellas of the
banyan trees.

Outside El Convento, the sixteenth-century convent
that had been restored as a hotel, a big table supported
a thousand-pound birthday cake. It was designed as a
Spanish garden with flowers and fences and a Felisa doll

on top, dressed in Popular Party colors, with pearls, the familiar halo braids, and a fan.

The party was for everyone who wanted to come. People who lived on the blocks around the square put little tables in front of their houses and brought out fried codfish cakes and *morcillos* and *chicherones* they had made. The orchestra played for hours. Then everyone went into the Cathedral for a special birthday Mass.

Some people begin to take it easy in their seventies. Looking at Doña Felisa's appointment book, one can see that it has not occurred to her yet.

She is up at six and sometimes in a meeting at seven. Often there is a visiting dignitary from the United States or Latin America to be shown around. Schools, hospitals, and housing projects in San Juan have all won international attention.

Felisa is proud to tour her city. She combines a tour with surprise inspection visits.

"Look," she tells the visitor. "They didn't know I was coming, but look how spotless this clinic is—how well it runs!"

A hospital visit with Doña Felisa takes time, for she stops to find out about the seriously ill, cheers them on, commiserates with their families, and leaves promising to pray for them.

She stops by a slum. A rich man is donating a swimming pool for the children and she must decide on a site for it.

"Las Mañanitas"

An old, old lady in a black shawl is grumbling. "Everything is for the young around here."

Felisa tells her, "I'll remedy that. One day a week, the pool will be reserved for old people."

The old lady cackles with pleasure. "Good! I'll get a bikini!"

Threading out of the slum, Felisa gives a ride to half a dozen children, then leans out to reproach a man whose roof boards are hanging loose.

"It costs nothing to hammer those boards on," she tells him. "Why spoil the view!"

He sheepishly agrees to repair it.

It is almost time for a reception for a literary award winner at City Hall. Felisa creams her face in the car and takes off her white turban. Underneath is a dressier turban. She takes off the jacket of her dress and is ready for the reception.

She leaves the reception early to attend a Model Cities meeting.

At night, there is a formal dinner, followed by three political meetings in three widely separated parts of town.

Her secretary looks at her watch. It is two A.M. Felisa must be tired. But as she comes out of the last meeting, a phonograph is playing and Felisa executes a little gay dance step to the music.

For twenty years, Felisa has been winning elections by a landslide. She is still bursting with energy. But there were seventy candles on her cake. . . .

Doña Felisa

"I'm going to retire," Felisa announces. "I will not run again. I want to read some books and go to the theatre for a change and spend some time with my family."

There is a hue and cry but she has made up her mind. "I will not run for mayor in 1968."

XVIII

———◆◼◆———

"Something from God"

IT WAS three A.M. when the pigs stampeded. Squealing and grunting and knocking into shacks, the whole herd charged up the hill in panic.

The people of La Perla sat up in bed and said, "What's the matter with the pigs?"

The matter was a wave. A tremendous, terrifying wave that had risen from the sea, swept in and broken over the row of houses that stood on stilts over the narrow, sandy beach. The pigs, sleeping in the sand among the pilings, shrieked in terror and headed for higher ground.

Lights began to come on in the slum as the big wave was followed by others. There had been no storm warning. The great waves were unannounced and unexplained. But they kept coming and getting higher. By morning, along the length of Puerto Rico's north coast, sea walls and overlooks were lined with people watching them. One of the watchers was the Mayor of San Juan.

"Call out the Civil Defense," she said, "and start evacuating La Perla."

There was still no storm. The sky was endlessly blue, the trade wind light and pleasant and the sun agreeably golden. But when the waves reached ten feet over normal, the first house in La Perla began to go. Khaki-clad Civil Defense men had the householders out, well in advance, and most of their worn furniture had been passed from hand to hand up the cliff to safety.

The waves were still growing. The rescue workers rushed to clear out more houses.

A *marejada*, they call it in Spanish—a battering of great waves.

"But what is it?" a tourist, standing on the overlook, asked a La Perlan. "A storm somewhere else? An earthquake under the sea?"

The La Perlan spread his hands. "Who knows?" he said. "*Algo de Dios.*" Something from God.

A great wave curled around the stilts of a board shack. The sticks broke and the house dropped down into the churning water, bobbing like a boat. Withdrawing, the wave pulled it out to sea. The next one brought it in again to crash and splinter against the rocks.

Felisa had the school at the top of the hill opened up for the evacuees. There were scores of them now. "Hot meals and dry clothes," she ordered.

Suddenly, the crowd yelled and surged forward. "The

fat man's house is going!" It was a big house, freshly painted salmon pink. The waves had knocked the front stilt out and the porch hung at a crazy angle. The owner and the Civil Defense workers struggled to get a big bed out and up the hill.

"Volunteers!" The bullhorn was blasting.

A dozen men and boys scrambled down the slope to run in and out saving the family's skimpy possessions.

Then, "All out! The engineer says all out!"

The helmeted engineer slammed the door and hammered a board across it so no one was tempted to go in for some last-minute treasure.

"*Esa es!*" the crowd shouted. "That's the one!" as a wave pounded in. It hit, boiling, and the fat man's house rose up on it, cracked into a hundred broken boards and dropped into the caldron below.

From another direction, "Everybody out!"

A woman was screaming, "No! No!" She couldn't leave her refrigerator. It was on installments. They got it out, but she still fought off the rescue workers. "No! No! Leave me here!"

Felisa's voice was on the bullhorn. "Come out!" she cried. "You are not alone! You will be taken care of! This is Felisa calling you. God gave us the power to help you. Don't risk your life down there. Come out!"

The woman stopped struggling. Her head turned, searching for Felisa in the crowd above. Then she let the Civil Defense man lead her out of danger.

Doña Felisa

"Esa es!" the crowd yelled as a wave took her house. At the top of the hill, Felisa was waiting for the woman. They embraced sorrowfully.

Hundreds were homeless. The Lincoln School had become a huge temporary encampment. Felisa went through the rooms, soothing parents, patting children, calming old people. She left for half an hour to appear at a reception for some foreign dignitaries. Wearing long earrings and a big orchid corsage, she returned and continued her rounds.

"Don't worry," she told people. "We are making arrangements. There will be a place for you in the new housing project."

To an aide she said, "They must not be rebuilt, these houses. Never so close again."

It was three A.M. when Felisa's limousine dropped her off at the City Hall. She rode the elevator up to her apartment.

In her small room, she took off the big orchid, admired it for a moment, then offered it on the shrine of Our Lady of Perpetual Help.

She slept fitfully. At five A.M., she had made a decision.

"It is settled. I will not run for Mayor again. I have announced it. That is finished."

But she was thinking. "Senator. I might still run for Senator, or if not that, there are other ways I could help."

"Something from God"

She looked at the clock. The night watchman liked a cup of coffee before he went home.

The Cathedral chimes were ringing the beginning of another day as the Mayor of San Juan went to the kitchen and put on coffee for the watchman.

Index

Index

ABOUT THE AUTHOR

MARIANNA NORRIS grew up in New York City and attended Barnard College. A job as "Around New York" reporter with the municipal broadcasting station led her into writing documentary programs. Subjects she has explored on the television networks range from bullfighting to child psychology, from rocketry to the mystery of Stonehenge. She has won the Peabody and Ohio State awards for television programs. Her films on life in America, written for the United States Information Agency, have been shown in over fifty foreign countries.

Miss Norris' extensive travels have resulted in such books as YOUNG TURKEY and YOUNG INDIA. She is well acquainted with Puerto Rico and has spent considerable time there interviewing personalities and doing research for this book and also for her previous one, FATHER AND SON FOR FREEDOM, the story of Muñoz Marín and his father, Muñoz Rivera.

Marianna Norris lives in New York City with her young daughter, Allegra.